Herbs &
SPICES
A Gourmet's Guide

THIS IS A CARLTON BOOK

ISBN 1 85868 712 8

Project editor: Camilla MacWhannell
Project art direction: Zoë Mercer, Diane Spender
Design & editorial: Iain MacGregor, Neil Williams and Ian Chubb
Production: Garry Lewis
Picture research: Lorna Ainger
Special photography: Howard Shooter

Printed and bound in Dubai

With special thanks to Debora Fioravanti for additional picture research, The Garden Picture Library, Jean Hosking at FLPA

PICTURE ACKNOWLEDGEMENTS
The publishers would like to thank the following sources for their kind permission to reproduce the pictures in this book:

AKG London 35, 38, 58, 60
courtesy Crabtree & Evelyn Ltd. 92b
et archive 41, 63
Mary Evans Picture Library 34, 36, 37, 56-7, 62
The Garden Picture Library/Linda Burgess 52-3, Brian Carter 43, David Cavagnaro 15, Erika Craddock 49, Geoff Dann 48, P.W. Flowers 4-5, 27, John Glover 23, Neil Holmes 50, Mayer/Le Scanff 12, 21, 40, Jerry Pavia 18, 19, 39, Howard Rice 20, Tim Spence 68
Robert Harding Picture Library 91/Trevor Wood 8-9
Image Select/Ann Ronan 59, 61, 73
Frank Lane Picture Agency/W. Broadhurst 11, Eric and David Hosking 16, Life Science Images 32-3, Wil Meinderts/Foto Natura 10, 51, Sunset 14, 44, 89, M.J.Thomas 45, G op net Veld/FotoNatura 86, Jan Vermeer/Foto Natura 26, Tony Wharton 13, 25, 42
Su-Lin Ong 28
Panos Pictures/Jeremy Horner 84
courtesy Sharwoods Ethnic Food Bureau 85
Howard Shooter 1, 3, 6-7, 46-7, 54-5, 64-67, 69-72, 74-75, 77-81, 83, 87, 90, 95
Tony Stone Images/Chris Bayley 17, 22, 24, Nicholas DeVore 82, Nick Dolding 88, Christel Rosenfeld 2, Jay S Simon 76
courtesy R.Twining and Company Ltd./EPR Ltd. 29

Every effort has been made to acknowledge correctly and contact the source and/copyright holder of each picture, and Carlton Books Limited apologises for any unintentional errors or omissions which will be corrected in future editions of this book.

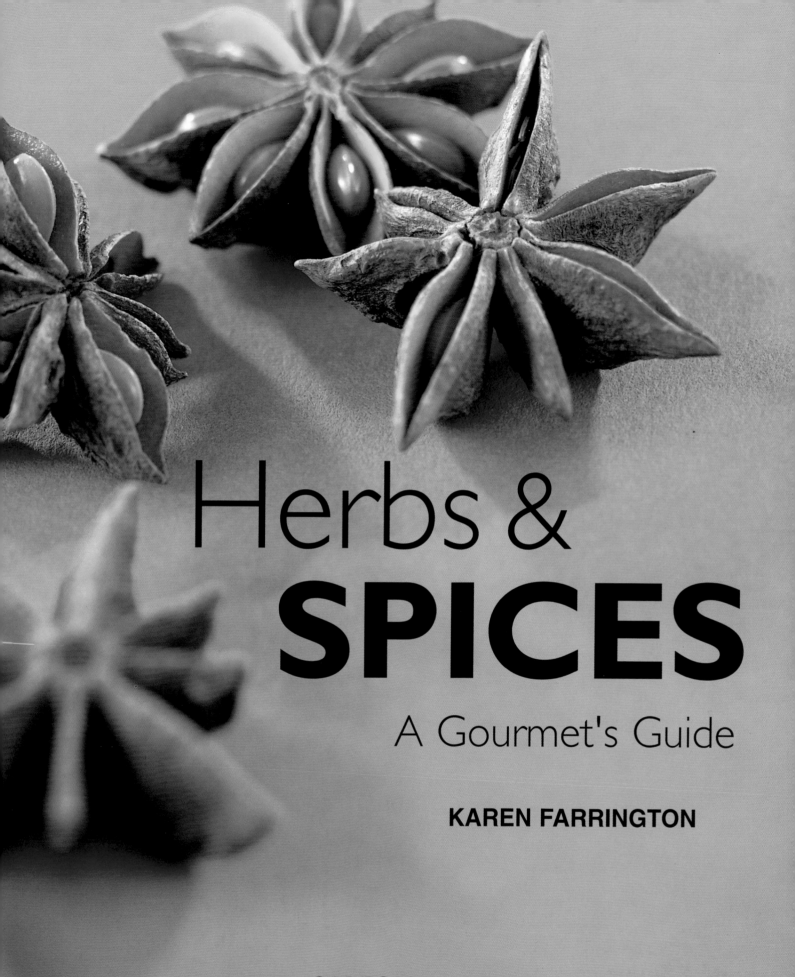

Herbs & SPICES

A Gourmet's Guide

KAREN FARRINGTON

CARLTON

CONTENTS

HERBS

To some, herbs are the crushed grey-green flakes in small glass jars lining supermarket shelves. To others they are the contents of the garden, the hedgerow and the fields beyond. According to the dictionary definition a herb is a plant which does not have a woody stem – one that withers in the first chill of winter. Rosemary plants do have a woody stem and they don't die when the cold weather comes, nor do bay trees conform to this strict definition, yet who would deny that both are herbs? Understanding of the word 'herb' is very much a personal matter but in most minds it is surely inextricably linked first to food and then to healing. It is for these twin purposes that herbs were first cultivated, perhaps even before the invention of the wheel.

HERBS IN
THE KITCHEN

Herbs provide us with many different flavours, from the delicate sweetness of angelica to the sour tanginess of sorrel. Utilising them can be as simple as chopping up mint for a sauce or as complicated as making one of the herbal liqueurs comprising of dozens of different herbs. However you apply them, herbs can impart a piquant flavour to the blandness of meals, improve an already tasty dish, or can even be used in a refreshing drink.

Chives

LATIN NAME   *Allium schoenoprasum*
FLOWERS   Purple, fading to pink
FOLIAGE   Grass-like and hollow

As the smallest sibling in the onion family, chives are indispensable in the kitchen for they impart a peppery yet mild flavour. The bulb is also edible and is likewise far less fierce than its big brothers.

In the garden chives soon make a clump which is easily divided. Promote growth by snapping off the flower buds.

Chives grow freely in the wild and there's a Chinese variety with large, flat leaves. This herb cannot be dried but may be frozen when cropping abundantly for use in the winter months.

Dill

LATIN NAME   *Anethum graveolens*
FLOWERS   Clusters of small, yellow blooms
FOLIAGE   Feathery

Dill is a dead ringer for fennel. Although dill is more compact it is easy to mistake the two, and special care should be taken in cultivation to keep the pair apart and so avoid cross-fertilisation.

Its flavour sets it apart from other herbs and it is used with fish, in pickling and in delicately flavoured sauces or butters. It is most often found in Scandinavian or central European cuisine. Both leaves and seeds are used.

Like fennel, it was once a remedy for gripey babies, and for the Greeks eating dill was a way of curing hiccoughs. Today the use of dill in medicines has diminished.

Angelica

LATIN NAME   *Angelica Archangelica*
FLOWERS   Greenish-white umbels
FOLIAGE   Sweet-smelling and serrated,
                              fresh green in colour

Hard to believe that the sugar-coated candies so beloved by cake decorators were once part of huge, large-leafed herbs swaying in the breeze. Crystallised angelica is made from the young stalks of the plant which are cut and covered in sugary syrup, simmered, cooled and then tossed in caster sugar.

There are other, less commonly known uses for angelica. Young shoots can also be used with stewed fruit or in jam while some cultures favour it cooked as a vegetable. Its leaves may be used in salads, but beware the distinctive flavour.

Its Latin name indicates just how valued it was in olden days for its sweetness. Traditionally its blossom appeared on the feast day of St Michael the Archangel.

Chervil

LATIN NAME   *Anthriscus cerefolium*
FLOWERS   Small and white
FOLIAGE   Feathery and fern-like

Chervil is valued for its light and sweet taste. In France it ranks highly in the herb garden, often taking the place of parsley in recipes. It has a similar appearance to parsley but the foliage is more delicate and a slightly paler green.

It does not dry well so eat chervil fresh from the garden in the early spring grown from seed sown the previous autumn, to reawaken the taste buds. It has a reputation as a spring-cleaning herb too, being well known for its blood-cleansing properties. In the summer it is best left uncooked and sprinkled over a salad. Don't forget to break off the flower heads when they appear to stop the chervil plant from bolting.

Celery and celery seeds

LATIN NAME   *Apium graveolens*
FLOWER   Grey-white
FOLIAGE   Fan-shaped in florets

There's more to celery than meets the eye. It is best known as a vegetable which was cultivated from the wild variety by Italians in the 17th century. Yet the wild herb still yields useful leaves which can be used in any recipe that cries out for that subtle celery flavour.

Further, there are small, brown seeds with a flavour more concentrated than both stalks and leaves. Left whole they can go into bread dough or be sprinkled over salad. When they are ground they can be used alongside salt and pepper.

Celery leaves and seeds are available dried.

CELERY AS A HERB SHARES A SIMILAR FLAVOUR TO ITS VEGETABLE NAMESAKE BUT THE SEEDS HAVE A STRONGER FLAVOUR.

Tarragon

LATIN NAME   *Artemisia dracunculus*
FLOWERS   White, bobbly flowers
FOLIAGE   Dark green and spikey

Few herbs have a reputation which precedes them in the same way as tarragon. It is adored by the French who insist upon it for their most exquisite sauces.

There are, in fact, two different types, French and Russian. It is the French variety that has the great chefs drooling. The Russian strain doesn't play on the tongue in the same way and it is often more sour than sweet.

Apart from the taste French tarragon has smoother, shinier leaves which are more widely spaced along the stem. Neither can be cultivated by sowing seeds – the flower heads are inadequate. Instead, propagate new shoots along the plant's coiled root. It is still sometimes known as the 'little dragon' because its leaves were once used to sooth animal and insect bites.

Borage

LATIN NAME   *Borago officinalis*
FLOWERS   Profuse purple/blue stars
FOLIAGE   Coarse, floppy, hairy

For sheer splendour, no herb garden should be without borage. Its flowers are dazzling and, as they are filled with nectar, a constant lure for bees and butterflies.

While some choose to cook borage leaves as a vegetable or add to a salad, its main use these days is in drink. Not only is it attractive but it lends a fresh, cucumber-like flavour. It is a must for a Pimm's No. 1, a popular warm-weather cocktail.

Whether it is because of its associations with drink – or perhaps the leaves do dispel depression – borage is said to make men merry. It is often called a 'herb of gladness' and the Greek proverb says: 'borage brings always courage'.

Marigold

LATIN NAME   *Calendula officinalis*
FLOWERS   Sunshine yellow through orange into rust
FOLIAGE   Various

These days marigolds have been relegated to nothing more than an eye-catching addition to the flower border. Our forefathers knew better, and used marigolds for multifarious purposes.

In the kitchen they used the petals in soup or to colour insipid butter or cheese. Petals were also used as a substitute for saffron, as a garnish for salad or in a soothing tea.

Medicinally, both flowers and leaves were made into lotions for wounds, boils, sprains and stings. In the garden the marigold attracts pollen loving insects which will help fertilise crops and keep aphids at bay.

BORAGE HAS ATTRACTIVE FLOWERS AND IMPARTS A SUMMERY TASTE WHEN USED IN DRINKS.

Coriander

LATIN NAME   *Coriandrum sativum*
FLOWERS   White or pale pink, on spindles
FOLIAGE   Similar to flat-leaved parsley

In 1597 Elizabethan botanist John Gerard published the following description of coriander in his *Herball or Generall Historie of Plants*: 'The common coriander is a very striking herb; it has a round stalk full of branches, two feet long. The leaves are almost like the leaves of parsley but later on become more jagged... the flowers are white and grow in round tassels like dill.'

Coriander came from the east and that is where it is still most prolifically used. Leaves, seeds, even roots, find their way into Indian and south-east Asian dishes. In northern Europe the seeds – often finely ground – feature in recipes more often than the foliage.

CORIANDER LEAVES AND SEEDS HAVE A PLACE IN THE KITCHEN AND ARE PROMINENT IN EASTERN CUISINE.

The flavour is musky citrus with subtle, secondary hints of aniseed. It has a noble heritage. Coriander was mentioned in ancient Sanskrit manuscipts, by the ancient Greek herbalists and in the Bible. Seeds were found in the tombs of the Pharaohs in Egypt.

Rocket

LATIN NAME   *Eruca vesicaria*
FLOWERS   Cream or white
FOLIAGE   Long, spinach-like leaves

Rocket has lost favour with cooks and gardeners in northern climates, perhaps because in the garden it is inclined to bolt quickly. In the warmer regions of the world, however, it remains a popular salad herb. In a

bowl of mixed leaves it is valued for its decisive peppery taste, the same quality that made it a favourite of Roman legionnaires. It will also tolerate being tossed in hot olive oil, after which it can be combined with any kind of pasta.

Fennel

LATIN NAME	*Foeniculum vulgare*
FLOWERS	Clusters of small yellow pinheads combining to form a broad plate
FOLIAGE	Blue-green feathers

A herb-cum-vegetable, fennel is known worldwide for its aniseed flavour. Apart from its digestive qualities, it has long been associated with improving human eyesight and as a remedy for stings. Nicholas Culpeper (1616–54) wrote: 'The seed boiled in wine and drunk is good for those that are bit with serpents, or have eat poisonous mushrooms.'

He regarded it as a wonder-herb 'as good for the breaking of wind... to provoke urine... to break and ease the pain of the stone... stay the hiccough... allay the heat and loathings of the stomach, and the gripings thereof... open obstructions of the liver, gall and spleen... and to ease the painful and windy swellings of the spleen... as also in gout and cramps.'

A gentle suggestion of aniseed comes from the fragile leaves. The seeds are more powerful. These two parts of the plant are now most commonly employed with fish dishes. An association between fennel and fish was made years ago when fishermen who added the herb which grew wild around the coastline to their dishes appeared to benefit from cast-iron digestive systems.

Once the celery-like stalk was thought to be the best bit. Today there are sweet varieties cultivated for the stalk bases which are used in Mediterranean cookery.

THE LEAVES AND SEEDS OF THE FENNEL PLANT BRING AN ANISEED FLAVOUR TO DISHES.

ABOVE: TODAY, HYSSOP, WITH ITS BITTER-MINT FLAVOUR, IS FOUND MORE OFTEN IN DRINKS THAN FOOD.

Hyssop

LATIN NAME   *Hyssopus officinalis*
FLOWERS   Spikes of blue/white/pink
FOLIAGE   Narrow green spears

The evergreen hyssop has a minty flavour but its bitter overtones have put it out of style with cooks. Young leaves nevertheless sit well in a salad and can be added to fruit pie before cooking. Bear them in mind for soups and stocks, too.

It has fared better in the world of drinks. Hyssop is used in the making of the liqueur Chartreuse and is often an ingredient of cocktails. Hyssop tea, made from tender tips and flowers, was long regarded as soothing for bronchial or asthmatic conditions.

This hardy perenniel makes the best of most soils and one plant will last for several years. It can be replaced by new ones grown from seeds or cuttings.

Lovage

LATIN NAME   *Levisticum officinale*
FLOWERS   Greeny yellow
FOLIAGE   Coriander-celery cross

From small beginnings lovage turns into a giant. Hollow-stemmed stalks protruding from the crown of one small root and a handful of dark green leaves soon top the five feet mark. Few herb gardens are large enough to accommodate more than one.

Yet lovage is an enormous asset. Just a few leaves in cooking will mimic the effect of a whole celery head so it's an easy and economical alternative.

In parts of Eastern Europe the roots are eaten as a vegetable while elsewhere the stalks are crystallised for cake decoration. Its nickname of love parsley comes from its use years ago as a love token and aphrodisiac.

RIGHT: SURPRISINGLY, ONE BAY LEAF IS SUFFICIENT TO LEND FLAVOUR TO ALL MANNER OF DISHES. SHRED WHOLE FRESH LEAVES BEFORE USE.

Bay

LATIN NAME	*Laurus nobilis*
FLOWERS	Petite and yellow-white
FOLIAGE	Leathery and dark green, shiny on its upper side

To the touch bay leaves feel like glossy card. It is difficult to credit that just one of these added to soup, stews and so forth will impart a strong and spicy flavour. No bouquet garni is complete without one.

The bay is a member of the laurel family and care should be taken never to confuse it with its poisonous relatives. In ancient Greek and Roman times bay was used to thread wreaths for the heads of heroes, athletes and poets. The beguiling scent from its oils which made it ideal for this purpose likewise assures it a place in the kitchen.

Bay leaves are frequently dried for kitchen use. For best results do not dry them in the sun or they lose their rich green colour. Instead, spread them between sheets of paper and keep them flat. Dried bay leaves can be added to a dish whole or crumbled.

Lemon verbena

LATIN NAME	*Lippia citriodora*
FLOWERS	Fronds of purple
FOLIAGE	Uniform green leaves on graceful, tall stems

A native of Chile, lemon verbena has become naturalised all over Europe, although it undoubtedly fares better in warmer climates than cold.

The scent from which the plant gets its name is in the leaves. Indeed, this zesty fragrance makes it a rival to lemon balm. Use lemon verbena for pot-pourri because of its long-lasting aroma. In small quantities leaves can be added as flavouring to fruit salad.

Lemon balm

LATIN NAME	*Melissa officinalis*
FLOWERS	Delicate white blooms
FOLIAGE	Veined green leaves, tinged with gold

As the name suggests, lemon balm is a herb with an ability to soothe and sweeten. Lemon balm was grown in the Mediterranean for hundreds of years before its calming qualities were discovered, however. The Romans and Greeks considered that the power of lemon balm to attract bees was sufficient to earn it a spot in the garden.

It was the Arabs who discovered it had medicinal benefits for those who were anxious, stressed or depressed. Today it is used as often in drinks as in meals, including cordials, teas and liqueurs. It can be used wherever lemon juice is added. Crush a leaf between forefinger and thumb to release the delightful citrus scent, and judge for yourself which dishes would benefit.

The mints

LATIN NAME	*Mentha*
FLOWERS	Purple/white
FOLIAGE	Shades of green

No herb garden would be complete without mint, a versatile herb for use in soups, sauces, drinks and desserts. However, gardeners have cursed mint as often as they have blessed it for it is highly invasive.

GARDEN MINT (BELOW) AND SPEARMINT (RIGHT) ARE TWO AMONG MANY DIFFERENT TYPES OF HERB WHICH HAVE FOUND FAVOUR SINCE ANCIENT TIMES.

Combat this tendency by always planting mint in a bucket.

In mythology, the nymph Minthe was changed into this herb by a jealous Proserpine. The Greeks associated it with strength and rubbed it over their bodies. In doing so they stumbled on one of the early male deodorants.

Mint is the umbrella term for a vast range. Spearmint and peppermint are the most common but there's also basil mint, apple mint, pineapple mint, Eau de Cologne mint and many more.

In its praise John Gerard wrote: 'Mint is marvellous wholesome for the stomacke. It is good against watering eies. It is poured into the eares with honied water.'

John Worlidge offered another testimony in 1688: 'Garden mints were universally used for sauces in Pliny's time, and much commended for their singular virtues, especially the young red buds in Spring, when a due proportion of Vinegar and Sugar, refresheth the Spirits and stirreth the Appetite and is one of the best Sallads the Garden affords.'

Red bergamot

LATIN NAME   *Monarda didyma*
FLOWERS   Scarlet
FOLIAGE   Dark green

Red bergamot, and its close relative purple bergamot, earned a place in history by providing an alternative tea for the Americans during their taxation dispute with Britain in 1773. In the hostilities that ensued as America sought independence, bergamot tea – refreshing, minty, calming on the nerves – was the chosen brew. It was better known as Oswego tea, named after an American fort.

Bergamot takes its Latin name from Spanish botanist Nicholas de Monardes and its anglicised name from the Bergamot orange as both plants share the same scent.

The rewardingly attractive bergamot, which is now available with different coloured blooms, likes a little bit of shade and a lot of water.

Sweet cicely

LATIN NAME   *Myrrhis odorata*
FLOWERS   Small, white flowers which together
                 form a globe
FOLIAGE   Fern-like fronds

The sweetness of the large, lacy leaf is one of nature's gifts which is often overlooked. In these days of weight-watching it can sweeten stewed fruits and pies without the needless addition of calories. It's easy on the teeth. In addition, both leaves and roots can be used as vegetables or with salads.

Once it was greatly valued, as Culpeper tells us: 'It is so harmless you cannot use it amiss.'

It is one of the first plants to emerge in spring and the last to die back. The leaves have a pleasant aniseed smell. Yet gardeners remain wary because of the thick roots which travel underground to form new plants hither and to.

Catmint

LATIN NAME   *Nepeta cataria*
FLOWERS   Purple
FOLIAGE   Silvery, serrated leaves

Although none too pleasant for humans, the scent emanating from this attractive plant drives felines to a frenzy. For this reason, derivatives of catmint (also known as catnip) are used to impregnate playthings for puss at the local pet shop.

Prior to this it was popular in tea as an aid to digestion and stomach complaints. It has also been smoked for its mild hallucinogenic qualities.

Basil

LATIN NAME   *Ocimum basilicum*
FLOWERS   Small white or purple whorls
FOLIAGE   Tender green or purplish

Culpeper and his cronies were, by all accounts, divided on the merits of basil. 'This is the Herb which all Authors are by the Ears about, and rail at one another like Lawyers,' he wrote in 1652. So strong was its aroma that herbalists once feared it could cause severe internal damage.

Today basil is surely a chef's greatest ally. Not only can it be used raw in salads but it can be cooked in all manner of dishes, the act of which releases still more flavour and a delectable aroma. To taste basil at its finest you could try it as an accompaniment to tomatoes or even in a pesto sauce made from pine nuts, Parmesan cheese, garlic and olive oil, and served with pasta.

Sweet basil first grew in the East where it was held to be sacred to the Hindu gods Krishna and Vishnu. After it was imported into Europe in the 16th century it became a staple of the Mediterranean diet. It is an annual plant.

Its cousin bush basil, which originated in Chile, is better suited to northerly climes and it was this variety which flourished in England during Tudor times.

Now the range of basil is stunning. In addition to the familiar green there is the small-leafed Greek basil, frivolous and frilly purple ruffle basil and the moody, dark opal basil. Don't leave it just to patio pots or window boxes. Keep some on an inside window sill where the heady smell will not only make your mouth water, it will also keep the flies away. Pinch out flower heads as they form to extend its life.

LEFT: SWEET CICELY, AS ITS NAME IMPLIES, IS A NATURAL ALTERNATIVE TO SUGAR.

BELOW: CATMINT HAS A FRAGRANCE TO LURE EVERY PET PUSS.

Marjoram/ Oregano

LATIN NAME   *Origanum marjorana, Origanum onites, Origanum vulgare*
FLOWERS   Mauve, white or pink, three to a stem
FOLIAGE   Green or golden, soft, furry

In essence, marjoram is the tamed form of oregano which grows freely on the pine-clad hillsides of the Mediterranean, where it is known as 'joy of the mountainside'. Young couples were once garlanded with it when they announced their engagement and women used to add marjoram to water to improve its scent for, as Culpeper testifies: 'Marjoram is much used in all odiferous waters, powders etc. that are to be used to ornament and delight.'

The leaves of both are excellent partners for tomatoes and are stock ingredients on pizzas, in pasta sauces, in soups, with meat, in stuffings or on vegetables.

Sweet or knotted marjoram has the most delicate flavour, pot marjoram is the hardiest and oregano the most popular, perhaps because it dries better.

Parsley

LATIN NAME   *Petroselinum crispum*
FLOWERS   White
FOLIAGE   Flat leaved or curly

The Greeks and Romans associated parsley with death rather than dinner – which is ironic as this herb in both its forms is bursting with health-giving vitamins and minerals.

The flat-leaved sort is better for cooking as its taste is more robust. Its frilly partner is pleasing on the eye and can be deep-fried to accompany fish dishes. Hamburg parsley, a close relation, is grown for its root which looks like a turnip and tastes like parsley mixed with celeriac. Parsley has earned new favour for its powers to mask the odour of garlic in food, through the action of its chlorophyll.

Rosemary

LATIN NAME	*Rosemarinus officinalis*
FLOWERS	Mauve/blue
FOLIAGE	Silver-green needles, prone to sprawling but capable of five feet of growth.

Thanks to its habit of proliferating at the coast the Romans christened the herb 'Dew of the Sea'. Bees throng to it, filling the highly scented shrub with life. Still, it was rosemary that was once used at funerals.

Although its aromatic spikes can be finely chopped it is better used by the branch. Cook a soup, joint of meat or vegetable with a sprig which can be tossed aside before serving, its flavour having infused the food. Rosemary twigs stripped of their spikes can be used as skewers for barbecues.

Rosemary partners most meats but its flavour is particularly complementary with lamb.

Sorrel

LATIN NAME	*Rumex acetosa, Rumex scutatas, Rumex patientia*
FLOWERS	Small and red appearing late in the season
FOLIAGE	Green, spear-shaped

The French are fond of sorrel. Unsurprisingly, it is French sorrel which they cherish, which has thicker, fleshier, crisper leaves than the English variety.

Its taste is sour and tangy like lemon and in France it is used in a soup or in a sauce to go with salmon.

Although abundant in vitamin C, sorrel should be taken in moderation. That vinegary flavour comes from oxalic acid which can be harmful if taken in great quantities. Savour the flavour in salads or in dressings which will pep up bland food. Don't plant it until you are sure you like it – once sorrel roots are established they are extremely difficult to eradicate.

ABOVE: PARSLEY, FRILLY OR FLAT, CONTAINS IMPORTANT VITAMINS AND MINERALS.

LEFT: OREGANO HEADS ARE IDEAL WITH ITALIAN FOOD OR WITH MEAT AND STUFFINGS.

Savory

LATIN NAME	*Sautereja hortensis,*
	Sautereja montana
FLOWERS	White/lilac/pink
FOLIAGE	Diminutive green leaves lined up
	along fleshy stalks

There are two varieties, summer and winter. The fairweather species is best grown from seed and has a finer texture. Winter savory is a perenniel tough enough to survive the cold with gutsy foliage and flavour. Both, however, are sufficient to do the work of salt and pepper on a meal and as such are invaluable for those on a salt-free diet.

Savory thrives in poor soil and Italian gardeners like to grow both types side by side. By tradition savory is served with bean and pea dishes. Not only does it aid digestion but the savory fully enhances the flavour of the beans.

Sage

LATIN NAME	*Salvia officinalis*
FLOWERS	Blue/purple spikes
FOLIAGE	Various

There are more than 750 types of sage that range from the age-old cook's choice to a South American variety with hallucinogenic powers that is used in ritual magic!

For centuries sage has been attributed with health-giving qualities. Its very name is derived from salveo, the Latin word for 'good health'. Proverbs found in cultures as diverse as Saxon England and Arabia confirm that sage was believed to be linked to a long life.

Striking but sometimes bitter sage is often used with fatty meats, historically because it was thought to aid digestion.

Tansy

LATIN NAME   *Tanacetum vulgare*
FLOWERS   Yellow buttons
FOLIAGE   Dark green and ferny

A herb steeped in history, the use of tansy has diminished considerably. Nowadays it is restricted to just a pinch of chopped tansy leaf in a salad. Once it was fêted as an effective insect repellent, long before the chemical alternatives were available. As such it was strewn over floors and rubbed on the skin of meat.

Tansy is on the menu at the Jewish passover. Years ago it was commonly used at Lent in pancakes which were called tansies, its bitterness prompting the eater to reflect on the sufferings of Christ.

In the garden it has amazing longevity. A survivor, it will endure adverse weather conditions while sending out underground shoots to form new plants.

Thymes

LATIN NAME   *Thymus vulgaris*
FLOWERS   Mauve
FOLIAGE   Various

Wild, cultivated, green, variegated – chalk-loving thymes have a hundred different faces. However, while many have a place in the garden only three are crucial for the kitchen; wild thyme, garden thyme and lemon thyme.

Taken from the Greek word for courage it came to signify bravery and stamina.

Thyme not only became popular in French cuisine but also as an emblem of the country's revolution 200 years ago.

For ease, strip the small leaves from the woody thyme branch by pulling it between the prongs of a fork. Use it with care – a small amount of pungent thyme goes a long way.

LEFT: SAGE COMES IN NUMEROUS VARIETIES AND IS USUALLY A GOOD PARTNER TO MEAT.

BELOW: USE A PINCH OF THYME RATHER THAN A FISTFUL.

Drying Herbs

Even when summer ends you don't have to give up on

herbs. Simply dry garden herbs at home.

To succeed in drying herbs, pick leaves or sprigs after the dew has disappeared. The aim is to dry the herbs swiftly to preserve as much colour, fragrance and flavour as possible. For those with enduring stems, gather a bunch and suspend them, stalk uppermost, in a warm, well-ventilated room. The temperature should be between 25 and 30 degrees centigrade. If the temperature is too high essential oils in the herbs will diminish. Consider using a garden shed, an airing cupboard or an attic. Avoid the garage because the smell of fumes will contaminate the greenery. Protect the drying herbs from dust contamination by cloaking them in a paper bag, with the open end near the herb tips to allow ventilation.

When the foliage can be rubbed from the stems – but before it has crumbled into dust – collect the dried herbs and store. Should you prefer a finer consistency,

the brittle foliage can be crushed with pestle and mortar, a rolling pin or in a coffee mill.

If the herbs are thoroughly dried and kept in dark, airtight containers, they will last for 18 months. Check after the first 24 hours for signs of condensation and continue the drying process on a plate or tray if necessary. Among the herbs which can be dried successfully are sage, thyme, rosemary, bay, marjoram and even lemon balm.

Take care when choosing plants to be dried for their seeds. The seeds must be ripe for flavour – but if

they are left too long the pods which hold them will burst and they'll be scattered. Tie a paper bag loosely around the body of drying seed herbs like dill or fennel for collection.

Larger, fleshier leaves like basil can be spread on sheets of muslim placed over cooling frames which will allow free circulation of air. Flowers, like marigolds or nasturtium, and roots can also be dried like this.

Some herbs, like parsley, are more successfully frozen than dried. Put a chopped tablespoon of the herb in a section of an ice-cube tray.

Bouquet garni

Bouquet garni – which translated from the French means 'bundle of herbs' – is a valued addition to stews, soups and so forth. The herbs can be fresh, secured into bundles with string, perhaps nestling within the curve of a celery stalk, or dried. Commercially, bouquet garni contain dried herbs and are sold in paper sachets which resemble tea bags. These can be home-made with swatches of muslim. Use one sachet or a small bundle for sauces and two or more, or a large bundle, for quantities of stew or soup.

DRIED HERBS CAN OFFER THE FLAVOURS OF SUMMER WHEN IT IS COLD AND DARK OUTSIDE. THE TECHNIQUES OF DRYING ARE QUICKLY MASTERED.

Herbs in Drinks

Herbs are constituents of some popular drinks. Herbal tea is a pleasing alternative to brown tea and coffee. A broad choice is available in teabag form on the shelves of supermarkets and health food shops.

I t is, of course, possible to make your own herbal tea. Use a warmed teapot and put in a selection of your favourite herbs. You can put in fresh or dried leaves, flowers and small seeds. Pour on hot water, letting the brew infuse for 10 minutes before pouring the first cup.

As a rough guide, use one ounce (25g) of dried herbs or three ounces (75g) of fresh to a pint (500 ml) of water, or mimic the ready-made herbal teas by putting herbs onto a small muslim square and tying it with string. Home-made herbal teas tend to be stronger and more bitter than milder, shop-bought varieties. Herbal tea can be sweetened with honey.

Herbs are also used in the making of liqueurs. Makers are notoriously secretive about the contents of their best-sellers but some facts have slipped out over the years.

Chartreuse, forest green or sunflower yellow, is one such drink. It was first made for medicinal purposes by monks at the Monastery of the Grand Chartreuse in the 17th century after an ancient recipe purporting to be an 'elixir of life' was presented to them.

In it were some 130 flowers, herbs, roots and spices – stock ingredients of the era. So popular was this tonic medicine the monks decided to sweeten it and sell it as a drink. In 1745 Green Chartreuse became available for the first time, followed almost a century later by Yellow Chartreuse. The monks still produce the liqueur at their monastery tucked away in south-eastern France.

A similar liqueur comes from Izarra in the Basque region of Spain, made from herbs of the Pyrenees. Another Spanish herbal liqueur is Cuarenta y Tres which contains 43 different plant parts.

In France Benedictine Brother Don Bernardo Vinvelli created a herbal liqueur in 1510 at Fecamp. It took the order's name.

In 1789 all production was stopped as the French revolutionaries repressed the country's abbeys. It was a century before production began again after the original recipe was by chance discovered. Benedictine contains the essence of 27 plants, including angelica, clove, cinnamon, vanilla, juniper and myrrh.

Strega, a liqueur from southern Italy, was first produced in 1860. The name translates to 'witch' and the brew is said to emulate the potions concocted by witches of the region.

GALLIANO, A POPULAR COCKTAIL INGREDIENT, HAS 40 DIFFERENT HERBS, ROOTS, BERRIES AND FLOWERS, ALL OF WHICH ARE CULLED IN THE ALPINE REGION.

Beauty Bonus

Herbs can give natural beauty a boost when they are applied by facial steam, face packs, bath oils or salts, eye baths, nail baths and hair rinses. As if to prove it, the majority of modern cosmetic companies champion their cause.

Key cosmetic herbs are lime flowers, which improve circulation and chase away wrinkles; salad burnet, a beautifier in baths; chamomile for its astringent and anti-inflammatory qualities; horsetail, an antiseptic astringent; peppermint, another antiseptic disinfectant; rosemary, a hair growth promoter; yarrow, for greasy skins; eyebright, in eye baths and compresses; elderflowers, a softener and cleanser; and fennel, considered particularly beneficial to eyes. The extensive list goes on and choices are made according to personal taste and efficacy.

Facial steams are inexpensive and effective. Put two handfuls of a chosen herb into a bowl and pour over two pints of boiling water. Make a tent over the bowl using a large bath towel, then use a second towel for extra insulation. Hold the previously-cleansed face under the towel where it feels comfortably hot for about ten minutes. Wash off the moisture from the skin with a cold, wet flannel. Do not go outside for at least an hour.

Ideal herbs for steamers are lime, lavender and nasturtium flowers, nettles, yarrow and salad burnet. Beware — facial steams are not advised for dry or veined skins or for people with heart and respiratory problems, including asthma. Face masks like those bought in shops can be quickly mimicked at home. Use a base like oatmeal, corn starch, yoghurt or similar, adding herbs where required.

In the bath

Herbs can be used at bath time both for cosmetic aid and as a great way of lifting the spirits. Add about ten ounces of dried herbs to a full bath and let it stand for ten minutes. For comfort, confine the herbs to a muslim bag which can be fixed under the running tap.

An infusion of rosemary is famed for bringing the shine back to lifeless hair. Henna can be used to rejuvenate dark hair, while chamomile highlights lighter hair. Apply both through an infusion.

FAR LEFT: ENJOY THE BEAUTY BENEFITS OF HERBS THROUGH INFUSED STEAM.

LEFT: ROSEMARY APPLIED THROUGH INFUSION HAS A REPUTATION FOR PRODUCING BEAUTIFUL, SHINY HAIR.

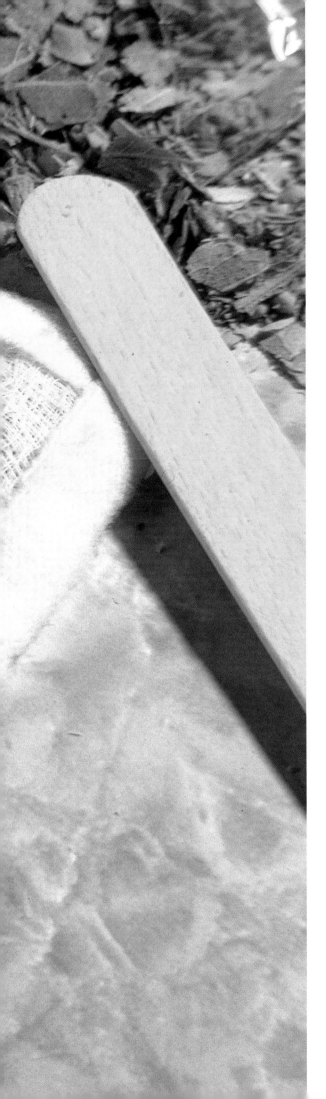

HEALING HERBS

In the modern era there are two schools of thought about herbal medicine. One condemns it as bunkum, the product of old wives' tales and superstition. The other trusts in the power of herbs, respecting the ancient wisdom of our folklore. Faith in the power of herbs grew at a time when people were far better attuned to nature and its gifts and, although no-one today would claim that ancient herbal remedies are foolproof, an increasing percentage of the population now believes that herbs do indeed have very real medicinal qualities.

Once people treated cuts by making an ointment of boar's grease and moss from the inside of a long-dead corpse's skull, and applying it with a knife. Thankfully, today's herbal remedies are considerably more palatable! However, Shakespeare coined the view of many then and now when he wrote in *Romeo and Juliet*:

'O Mickle is the powerful grace that lies
In herbs, plants, stones and their true qualities:
For nought so vile that on earth doth live
But to the earth some special good doth give,
Within the infant rind of this weak flower
Poison hath residence and medicine power.'

History of Medicinal Herbs

Since ancient times the sheer variety of available herbs has exploded. Once mankind knew only the herbs that grew in the immediate neighbourhood. Later, when transport afforded him the opportunity to venture further, he found new herbs which required different weather and soil conditions to flourish than those he knew before. Exploration overseas increased the number of known plants manifold.

The hunter-gatherers who wandered on earth centuries ago were the first to experiment with herbs. We'll never know just what prompted them to sample plants and how they distinguished the delicious from the downright dangerous. This was a brave, new world in which the bold tasted herbs which even today grace our tables. They also ate herbs which are nowadays strictly for show, and still more which are long forgotten.

As their understanding of plants expanded they discovered that some appeared to cure their internal ailments or heal external wounds. Before long special significance was attached to such plants, hallucinogenic herbs particularly so. Illnesses were considered the product of supernature and the curative plants were

NATIVE PEOPLES BECAME EXPERTS ON THE MEDICINAL QUALITIES OF HERBS GROWING IN THEIR VICINITY.

thought magical, as were the circumstances in which they were harvested and prepared.

Superstitions which sprang up about herbs endured for generations. St John's Wort was considered an aid against nervous disorders – but only if it was picked on Midsummer's Eve. Vervain would staunch blood from open wounds – if it was picked during particular phases of the moon *and* while the picker chanted an appropriate series of spells.

Ridiculous the superstitions might now seem, but it was hard to explain why small, often fragile plants had any munificent power. Even today science has difficulty in defining why some plants apparently have healing properties, and ancient instincts have often been proved sound.

The Indians of Peru used the ground bark of the cinchona tree to cool a fever. Not until the 17th century did medics discover that quinine was in the cinchona tree, which can be used to alleviate malaria.

Herbalists once used minute quantities of the poisonous foxglove plant to treat heart maladies. Much later doctors praised the properties of digitalis in the treatment of heart complaints. It was, of course, an extract from the foxglove.

ONCE HERBS WERE GROWN AS MUCH FOR THEIR CURATIVE ABILITIES AS FOR AN ADDITION TO COOKING.

The Advance of Herbalism

Greeks who dealt in medicinal herbs were devotees of Asclepius (or Aesculapius), the Greek god of medicine. The chaste and learned Asclepius was a son of Apollo and was acclaimed as a miracle worker. Ultimately he was struck dead by a thunderbolt issued by Zeus after the healer defied the king's wishes. The sick would frequently seek 'sleep cures' by bedding down in the temples of Asclepius at Epidaurus and on the island of Cos, believing the god would heal through dreams.

There was a school of medicine founded in Alexandria in 332 BC by the Ptolemies where an ancient 'database' was built up, with soldiers bringing back information on herbs and their uses from across the empire established by Alexander the Great. Alas, all the valuable work done on behalf of the Medical School of Alexandria was lost when the place was burned down by a mob of Christian fundamentalists in 391 AD.

The Romans were less enamoured with the arts of healing. Greek doctors who travelled to Rome were virtual outcasts until Julius Caesar conferred on them the rights of Roman citizenship in 46 BC.

Progress was eclipsed by the Dark Ages. Still, even during those times herbs were valued by the monks and were cultivated behind monastery walls. A monastery at St Gall in Switzerland had 16 herb beds by the year 830. The Middle Ages brought about a revival of interest. Writers like John of Gaddesden, an English monk, and the German Konrad von Megenberg

ASCLEPIUS, THE GREEK GOD OF MEDICINE, DISCOVERS THE MAGICAL HERB BETONY.

NICHOLAS CULPEPER
(1616–54), HERBALIST.

bequeathed manuscripts which revealed the growing trend towards herbal remedies during the 14th century.

But advances in herbalism were dogged by magic and superstition, both widely peddled at the time.

Even well-respected herbalists were way off beam. Many subscribed to the Doctrine of Signatures in which body parts were treated with herbs which resembled them. William Coles, author of the *Art of Simpling* published in 1656, explains: '(God) stamped upon them (plants) – as upon every man – a distinct forme but also given them particular signatures whereby a Man may read even in legible Characters the Use of them. Heart Trefoyle is so called not only because the Leafe is

triangular like the Heart of Man, but also because each Leafe contains the perfect Icon of an Heart and its proper colour.' Likewise, birthwort, with womb-shaped flowers, was given to women in childbirth.

Nicholas Culpeper not only adhered to the doctrine but concerned himself with the sun, moon and planetary positions and their relation to herbs. His *Herball*, otherwise known as *The English Physician*, was a best-seller. It was his intention that, through it: '...a man may preserve his body in health; or care himself, being sick, for three pence charge, with such things only as grow in England, they being most fit for English bodies.'

The Apothecary

The 15th century was characterised by exploration, increasing the number of herbs under scrutiny, and the advent of printing through which more information than ever before could be disseminated.

It was the age of the apothecary. At first apothecaries were sellers of drugs, purchasing their supplies from people who scoured the countryside for the necessary roots and leaves. But in time their role became increasingly diagnostic, for no-one had a better notion of which herb to use for which sort of ailment.

Apothecaries, who had been attached to the Grocer's Company by way of professional allegiance, formed their own Worshipful Society of Apothecaries of London in 1617, with 114 members.

Apothecaries and later physicians ultimately planted physic gardens to furnish themselves with supplies of herbs.

The advent of modern medicine batted herbalism into the outfield once more. Plant-based drugs – even

A HERB GARDEN OF THE MIDDLE AGES, WITH A DOCTOR SELECTING HERBS FOR MEDICINAL PURPOSES.

proven ones like morphine and quinine – gave way to man-made drugs. Herbal remedies were relegated to fringe status, which is where they have remained.

Pharmaceutical companies make synthetic drugs by the million from chemical formulae which have been through a cycle of trials. These are analytical times and doctors who prescribe these drugs are obviously delighted to know which compounds are efficacious. Still, the process of uncovering the hidden power of herbs has continued. In 1950 scientists

discovered that the Madagascan periwinkle (*Catharanthus roseus*), a run-of-the-mill jungle carpeting plant, contained not one but two drugs vital in the fight against cancer. It is farmed in Texas, America, where the bloom harvest is in excess of 17,600 lbs or 8,000 kg. Attempts to mimic the drugs synthetically have not yet met with success.

Sweet cicely is out of favour as a herbal remedy but may yet yield a drug called podophyllotoxin for use in the war on cancer.

Most herbal knowledge was divined in the centuries before experiment and control. It is possible that some herbal remedies work only as a placebo, i.e. people literally 'think' themselves well.

However, the following statistic is worth bearing in mind. There are 250,000 known plant species in the world. In 1988 only 90 species were used in the production of chemical compounds for clinical practice. By any measure, the world of medicine still has much to discover.

THE MADAGASCAN PERIWINKLE.

The Herbal Medicine Chest

The dilemma of herbal medicine today is exemplified by the recent fanfare arrival of kava onto world markets.

Kava, a relative of the pepper, has long been used in the South Seas as a relaxant. Indeed, in 1769 the explorer Captain James Cook witnessed Polynesian virgins chewing the firm root into a pulp before emptying the contents of their mouths into coconut milk which would duly be drunk by fellow islanders. It appeared a thoroughly repugnant practice – but that didn't stop the islanders. They enjoyed what they perceived to be the relaxing, mood-enhancing properties of the herb.

More than 220 years later herbal companies decided to make kava big news. A concerted advertising campaign in America resulted in pills, drops and teabags containing kava selling like hot cakes. The herb appears to work where anti-depressants fail – and there are no side effects to wrestle with.

Immediately the general public falls into two camps. One believes the circumstantial evidence which suggests kava is an equal of Valium in the treatment for anxiety. The other opinion declares that this reputation alone is insufficient to constitute proof. Until exhaustive tests have been carried out they claim kava has no place in modern medicine. After all, they say, there has not even been any long-term testing to prove that kava is safe. Perhaps they are victims of the age of reason who are repelled by anything that cannot readily be explained scientifically.

Although herbal remedies are direct products of nature that does not mean that they are without hazards. A patient may be allergic to a plant or a substance within it which will produce an adverse reaction. Getting the dosage right is just as important as with synthetic drugs.

There follows a list of herbs and the health benefits attributed to them. Remember, there are many ways to take herbs. There are infusions or tisanes, poultices, inhalation through steam baths, pills or syrups, ointments, powders, gargles, massage oils or the application of fresh leaves. Use all methods with extreme caution if pregnant.

Basil

It is something of an all-rounder. Basil, once used as a snuff, is recommended for colds and headaches. With acclaimed digestive properties basil has been used for gastric problems, constipation, as a sedative and to soothe fevers. Further, it is reputed to stimulate milk production in nursing mothers.

Bay

Now restricted to culinary use, bay was once used internally for digestive disorders and externally for the effects of rheumatism.

LEFT: BASIL HAS A MULTITUDE OF HEALING PROPERTIES, MAKING IT ONE OF THE MOST VERSATILE MEDICINAL HERBS.

BELOW: CAPTAIN COOK (1728–79) EATING WITH TAHITIANS.

Chickweed

Sometimes known as starweed, this is a herb for all seasons. In the spring it alleviates hay fever, in the summer skin problems. Come the damp of autumn it can work on rheumatism, while in the cold of winter it will aid bronchial sufferers and those with poor circulation. In addition it is said to assist in the treatment of blood poisoning, boils, piles, impotence, constipation and sore throats. It is equally at home in the kitchen as in the medicine chest.

Echinecea

The dried root in a tincture appears to raise the body's threshold against infection. Its antiseptic qualities have made it useful in the treatment of boils, acne, abscesses and tonsillitis.

Ashwagandha

Winter cherry, as it is otherwise known, is used in India to enhance male libido. In the West it is recommended as a tonic for the elderly and the chronically ill. The roots and the leaves are used. There are at least six species which grow in India, the Middle East and countries around the Mediterranean.

Yarrow

The flowers, leaves and essential oils from the yarrow plant are said to soothe allergies, reduce inflammation and staunch blood flow. Indeed, anyone suffering a nose bleed was once advised to stick a yarrow leaf up their nostrils. At least one of its varieties was known as 'sneezewort', 'the herbe that procureth sneezing'. In the treatment of colds it was said to 'bring mightely forth the slimy flegme from the brain'.

Coltsfoot

Once coltsfoot was used to treat everything from worms to the plague. Taking its name from its hoof-shaped leaves, it is nowadays more confined to the treatment of neuralgia.

Agrimony

Yellow spikes of agrimony at the peak of blooming and the accompanying serrated leaves may be helpful for stomach upsets or food allergies. It is also used to alleviate sore throats, catarrh and for the bathing of external wounds.

Meadowsweet

An extract of this frilly yellow plant formed the basis of aspirin in the 1830s. As an anti-inflammatory aid it has been used in the fight against rheumatism and can soothe stomach upsets.

Solidago

The Saracens used this plant to heal wounds during the Crusades and won it the name 'Heathen Wound Herb'. It is also thought helpful in the treatment of kidney problems.

RIGHT: CERISE QUEEN, OTHERWISE KNOWN AS YARROW.

BELOW: SOLIDAGO, ALSO KNOWN AS GOLDEN ROD, IS USED FOR WOUNDS AS WELL AS FOR KIDNEY AND BLADDER COMPLAINTS.

ABOVE: THIS DISTINCTIVE TREE BEARING ALOES GROWS IN GREECE, BARBADOS AND SOUTH AFRICA.

RIGHT: ELDERBERRIES ARE SAID TO CURE THE COMMON COLD.

Chamomile

The attractive white, bobbing flowers of chamomile are better known these days dried in the form of tea. Chamomile tea was heralded as the great, natural relaxant. Apart from its qualities as a sedative it can act against inflammation and bacteria. Culpeper thought it a cure-all: 'If the part grieved be anointed with that oil, taken from the flowers, from the crown of the head to the sole of the foot, and afterward laid to sweat in bed, and he sweats well.'

Aloes

Centuries ago this drug was regarded so highly that Aristotle asked Alexander the Great to conquer the island of Socotra, where it was grown, to ensure a ready supply. Today there are an additional two famous sources, Barbados and the African Cape. It has been used for digestive difficulties and also to heal burns.

Nettles

Widely regarded as a problematic weed, it was once essential in cloth manufacture. The young leaves are high in iron and minerals which together are a tonic for the anaemic. They also contain a natural salt. Nettles lose their sting when they are boiled or dried.

Rosehips

These bold orange buttons which decorate the countryside in the autumn are rich in vitamin C. They are also said to benefit the kidney and act as a diuretic.

Lady's Mantle

Reflecting its name, lady's mantle was used for problems associated with women's reproductive organs. It is largely ignored today.

Mugwort

A known digestive, the buds of mugwort were often used to season fat meat. Before the use of hops, it was also used in the making of beer. Mugwort tea was once used against rheumatism.

Elderflowers/Berries

Both flowers and berries of this prolific tree are accredited with purifying the blood. The flowers, in a tea, are said to be cold cures, while the berries can help those with sciatica and neuralgia.

Vervain

A plant held in awe by Greeks, Romans, Celts and Germanic tribes, it was frequently used in the magic/medicine which prevailed before the Dark Ages. Less revered these days, it has been used in the treatment of nervous disorders, the menopause, hay fever and skin complaints.

Hemp

The jury remains split over whether hemp, or cannabis as it is better known, is beneficial to the sick. It was recorded five centuries BC among Chinese herbalists and was used in medicine before being listed as an illegal narcotic. Its other uses include the making of rope and sailcloth.

GARDENER'S DELIGHT

'As is the garden so is the gardener.

A man's nature runs either to herbs or weeds.'

Francis Bacon (1561–1626)

Never before has there been so much help and advice available to start cultivating your own herbs. If you've ever bought lush green pot herbs from the supermarket and stood them on your windowsill at home to pick as you please then you have experienced the joy of having fresh, fragrant herbs on hand to turn a good dinner into a great one. Already, you will be sold on the idea of growing your own.

Grow from seed
Basil, parsley, dill, angelica, chervil, borage, caraway, cumin, foxglove, sunflower, coriander, sweet cicely, salad burnet and corn salad.

Divide
Yarrow, lady's mantle, wormwood, chicory, tarragon, lungwort, bergamot, catmint, tansy, periwinkle and comfrey.

Take cuttings from
Tarragon, juniper, bay, rosemary, lavender, rue, sage and coltsfoot.

Borders

For the purposes of gardening many more plants – apart from those grown for the kitchen or the medicine chest – fall into the classification of herbs.

The methods of propagation are various. Some sprout from seed fast and furiously, while for others it is a lengthy process. The alternatives, broadly speaking, are root division, in which a healthy and flourishing clump of the herb is split, or to take cuttings.

Some herbs, including chamomile, hyssop, lovage, mints, pennyroyal, mugwort and the thymes, can be cultivated by all three methods.

In a garden with sufficient space for a herb border, the scope is endless. Spend long winter evenings in front of the fire planning the border with due consideration for colour, foliage and the reason why each herb has a

ABOVE: A CARTWHEEL – THOUGH HARD TO COME BY – MAKES AN IDEAL SELF-CONTAINED HERB GARDEN.

RIGHT: SUNKEN HERB BEDS ONCE GRACED ALL THE GRAND HOUSES OF EUROPE.

place. There's no point in planting rosemary at the back of the border, for example, as you will end up trampling down other flowers to reach it.

An otherwise plain path down a garden can come alive with herbs. Many release a heavenly scent when they are crushed and are none the worse for it. A favourite from Victorian times is chamomile which can be planted as a lawn, and pennyroyal has the same qualities. Herbs are a big draw for bees and butterflies too, another bonus for a border. While scented gardens are an asset for all they become a must if someone in the household is visually impaired. Herbs are the perfect plot-fillers as their foliage is frequently compelling to the touch as well as the sense of smell.

Herbs which would suit a garden for the blind include angelica, chamomile, feverfew, scented-leaf geraniums, hyssop, meadowsweet, the mints, rosemary, sage, sweet cicely, tansy and thymes.

Herbs grown for perpetual use or for their roots are better placed in the vegetable garden. They will thrive in rows between other root crops where they can be easily harvested.

These days cartwheels are hard to come by. Once discarded ones were used for making quick-fix herb gardens, with the spokes acting as borders between each variety instead of hedges. It is still possible to achieve the same effect by dividing a circle of garden into segments, using tiles or wood as dividers.

Patio Pots

The main options for the small scale herb gardener comprise of troughs, patio pots, window boxes or hanging baskets.

Few can resist the Italian feel of trailing herbs in terracotta pots or troughs. Not all herbs will be successful in pots, however. For best results restrict the choice to borage, catmint, chamomile, chives, coriander, dwarf lavenders, lemon balm, marigolds, rosemary, sage and thymes.

For pots the name of the game is impact and the way to achieve this is through foliage rather than flower. Contrast herbs with dark green, light green, golden and grey leaves for best effect. If the pot lacks an architectural quality, pop in something like a spider plant which, with its variegated spikes, will be something of a crowning glory.

Try planting pots with just one herb, for example, mint. The effect of a medium-sized herb like mint is far greater when it is planted singly. A pot will also stop this notorious rampager from taking over your plot. In fact, mint is an unsuccessful partner in pots as it is prone to taking over. Another eye-catcher is the variegated lemon balm. Any foliage with contrasting colours will work just as well.

Only the tidiest of herbs are recommended for window boxes. Make the wrong choice and all natural daylight will soon be blotted out by rampant growth. Consider basil, parsley, chives, corn salad, sage, the thymes, nasturtium and perhaps a downward-travelling catmint for foliage variation.

Use gritty compost in the windowbox and don't forget to put crocks or polystyrene in the bottom to aid drainage.

A hanging basket crammed with herbs is another option. It looks good, it smells exotic and it tastes divine! Don't expect the same kind of yields that you might get if the plants were in open ground. Also you may not feel inclined to tamper with a stunning display for the sake of your lunch. But the foliage is easy on the eye and makes a welcome change from bold-as-brass begonias or petunias.

Its content is garnered only by your imagination. For best results, choose a deep basket that has been lined with moss or an artificial alternative. As a guide, for a 15-inch wide basket use a variegated sage, a thyme, a santolina and two chives – these diminish rapidly in the salad season. Put a neat lemon mint in, too, but keep it in a four-inch pot to contain its growing habits.

Keep the basket well watered and feed it regularly.

ABOVE: KEEP POT HERBS BY THE BACK DOOR FOR FREQUENT USE.

LEFT: A HANGING BASKET PLANTED WITH HERBS IS GOOD TO LOOK AT AND GREAT TO EAT.

Knot Gardens

Before the age of exploration European gardeners had only native plants for their plots. Herbs had special importance not just as edible crops but for ornamental purposes as well.

The knot garden is a tribute to herbs. The intricate knot patterns which the Tudors and Elizabethans took to their hearts were successful only because of the agreeably compact growing habit of herbs and their colours.

Knots were square gardens, often set side-by-side in groups of 12 or 16, but each with individual points of interest. The patterns were geometric or in the style of letters or emblems.

In those days the word 'knot' meant both an heraldic badge and 'to shear'. And indeed the knot patterns did reflect the intricacies of heraldry and were closely cropped.

The lines of the knot were interwoven, appearing to pass under and above one another. Each thread was a different colour, either shades of green or silver. The spaces between the threads were filled with coloured sand, gravel or batches of one particular flower.

So knot gardens were low growing and best appreciated from above. They were also labour-intensive, since to keep the herbs in good order, they had to be clipped at least monthly. The clippings were strewn over the floors of the big houses as a kind of walk-on, walk-off room freshener.

Knot patterns were also seen on floors, doors and stained glass windows. From the knot garden came the fashion for garden mazes and, later, the French-style parterres, low-growing and extensively patterned gardens like those at Versailles.

The most famous knot garden to survive is the one at Hampton Court Palace, which appears today much as Henry VIII, the palace's most famous resident, once saw it. A contemporary painting of King Henry in the garden shows another formal addition – heraldic beasts affixed on posts which are linked with stripped railings. The bill for the artwork still exists, dated 1533: 'To Henry Blankeston for paiting 960 yards of rail wite and green, the yard 6d' (two and a half pence).

Recreate a knot garden using box, lavender, thymes, sage, rosemary and winter savory. Any low-growing plant that has a tendency to 'mat' and can tolerate regular pruning is ideal.

KNOT GARDENS ARE DYNAMIC PATTERNS INSPIRED BY HERALDRY WHICH ARE BEST VIEWED FROM ABOVE.

SPICES

While herbs are generally perceived to be the leafy parts of a plant, spices are taken from the root, bark, flower, seed pod and seed. Generally spices are native to hot countries and they are dried to prolong their shelf life.

Spices are invariably strongly flavoured – that's why they are used – so they are ideal to accompany food which has a limited or unexciting flavour of its own. In small quantities spices have little nutritional benefit, but since they can be used to replace salt this alone can contribute to a healthier diet. Using spices effectively is a case of trial and error – use too much and they are a force to be reckoned with! Nevertheless, don't avoid them out of fear, for the cook who masters spice will have happy diners indeed.

THE STORY OF SPICE

There's little rarity value to spices today. Modern cultivation methods and transportation means that there are plentiful supplies to be shipped worldwide. But it wasn't always so. Once spices had a value akin to precious metals. People travelled the globe, fought wars and won and lost fortunes, all in the name of spice. According to Assyrian legend the gods drank wine made from sesame the night before they created earth. This may be a fanciful tale but there's plenty of evidence to prove that spices were around in ancient times and had already attained some importance in people's lives.

At the Great Pyramid there are hieroglyphics which reveal workers ate garlic for strength. In the Bible, Joseph was sold by his envious brothers to a band of travelling spice merchants bound for Egypt. Later, the Queen of Sheba numbered spices among her gifts to King Solomon. Spices were most used in the ancient world as preservatives, perfumes and medicines.

The Spice Trade

The spice trade was for centuries the domain of the Arabs who travelled in their camel caravans along a trade route which became known as 'the Golden Road of Samarkand'. It was another name for the famous Silk Road which spanned some 4,000 miles (6,400 kilometres) and linked China and Rome and numerous kingdoms between. Samarkand, which is now in Uzbekistan, became an important junction, being half-way between the chief destinations of east and west.

BELOW: THE SCHOLARLY PLINY THE ELDER WHO STUDIED ART AND NATURE IN 37 VOLUMES CALLED *HISTORIA NATURALIS* WAS SUFFOCATED BY THE FUMES OF A VOLCANO ERUPTION.

When the Romans came to prominence they fell victim to the Arab monopoly. An irate Pliny the Elder complained that the Arabian stranglehold left Romans paying 100 times the original cost of the spices. Romans mainly used spices in cooking.

Soon the Romans sought a share in the lucrative spice trade. Intrepidly, they embarked on two-year voyages from Egypt to India in order to reach supplies.

When they returned across the Indian Ocean they brought with them pepper, cinnamon, nutmeg, cloves and ginger. During the first century AD the Greek sailor Hippalus took note of the consistency of the winds in different seasons and found that during the summer months the winds blew in the direction of the south-west while in winter it was in reverse. By using the winds to their best advantage the ships were able to slash their travelling time to less than 12 months.

Still the shortage of supplies kept spices a sought-after luxury. A year's supply of cinnamon was ostentatiously burnt at the funeral of Nero's wife in 65 AD as a mark of respect.

Rampaging Goths demanded the unlikely ransom of 30,000 lbs of peppercorns – along with gold, gems and silk – to spare the population of Rome from slaughter after they invaded in 410 AD.

CAMEL TRAINS WERE THE TRADITIONAL METHOD OF TRANSPORTING PRECIOUS SPICES FROM THE EAST.

Eastern Tastes Begin to Spread Westwards

With the fall of the Roman empire, the spice trade fell into the doldrums until the Muslim empire emerged after the eighth century, when the prosperous trade routes were re-established. The Caliphs inspired a fresh approach to medicine, science, art and literature in the east, while the west stagnated through the Dark Ages. At their banquets the inspiration was spice.

In the Middle Ages Europeans acquired a liking for spices which masked the blandness of their tasteless food, and there was increasing pressure to open up new routes to provide more supplies at a competitive price. Venice, an independent republic, was by now the spice capital of the world, where traders bought and sold at hefty prices. It was a wealthy and successful city with a fleet of ships which helped bring defeat to its bitter rival, Genoa, in 1380.

The city was, however, put in the shade in the 16th century when new routes were opened up by Spanish and Portuguese explorers.

Christopher Columbus (1451–1506), an Italian sailing under the Spanish flag, embarked on his three major voyages in the final decade of the 15th century.

He landed in the West Indies and returned with allspice, vanilla, red peppers and many more great discoveries, although of course his financiers had hoped that he would reach the Spice Islands rather than stumble upon an unknown continent.

In 1498 Vasco da Gama (c1469–1524), from Portugal, was the first to sail around the Cape of Good Hope in southern Africa to reach Calicut, the busiest port on the Malabar coast of India. Also, the fleet of Ferdinand Magellan (1480–1521), a Portuguese navigator heading a Spanish expedition, encountered the East Indies before completing the first circumnavigation of the world.

LEFT: THE PORTUGUESE EXPLORER VASCO DA GAMA.

RIGHT: AFTER MARCO POLO RETURNED TO VENICE FROM FARTHEST ASIA HE WAS JAILED BY THE RIVAL GENOESE AND WROTE HIS FAMOUS MEMOIRS IN CAPTIVITY.

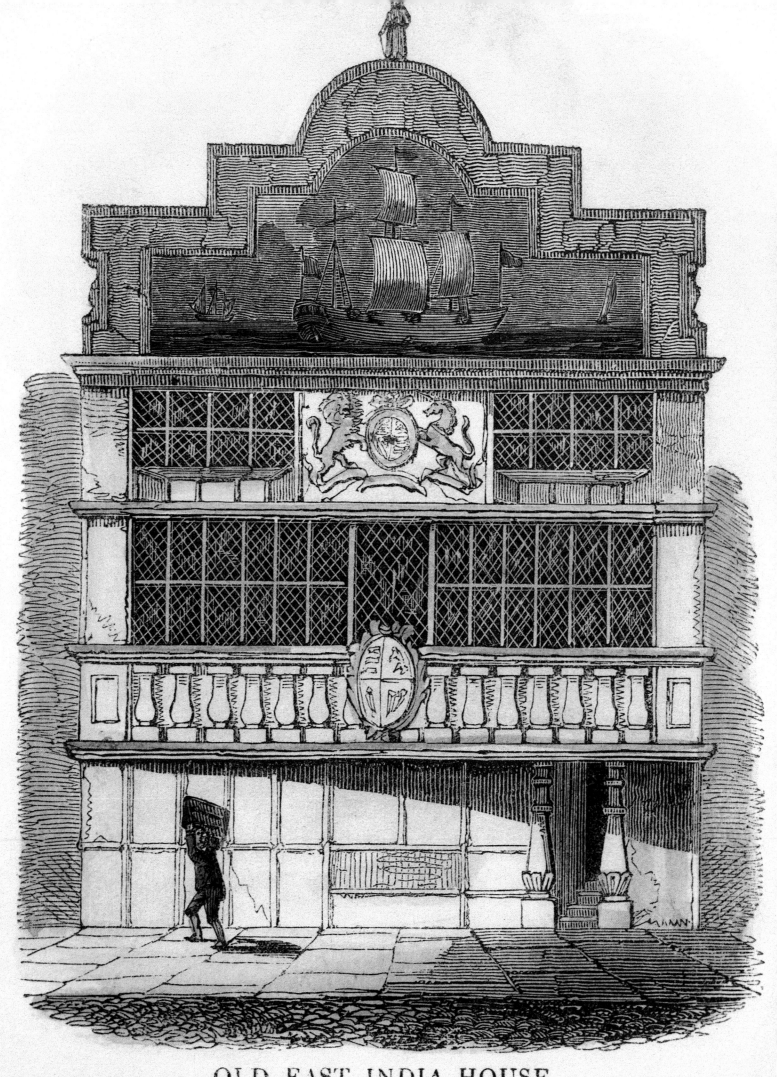

OLD EAST INDIA HOUSE.

The Seafaring Nations Take Control

For centuries it was powerful seafaring nations who were the masters of the spice trade. Portugal wrested control of the Spice Islands – the Moluccas, in Indonesia – from the Muslims and stocked up by bartering with the bemused islanders. Its capital, Lisbon, was the world's spice capital during the 16th century.

Within a century Portuguese dominance gave way to the empire-seeking Dutch. Their rule in the Spice Islands was far more barbaric than their predecessors and, by planting groves of sought-after spices, they deprived the islanders of food. Such was the increase in supply that spices were ultimately burnt on the streets of Amsterdam to avoid a collapse in the market.

The English were also casting envious eyes on the lucrative spice trade and joined forces with the Dutch in 1619 to fend off Portuguese and Spanish competition. As Dutch strength increased so did their sphere of influence, extending ultimately to Ceylon and its cinnamon trade and the pepper ports of western India. But their power came to an end in a two-pronged assault. After 1770 espionage by botanist Pierre Poivre brought important seeds out of the Spice Islands and into French-controlled tropical islands. Ten years later the Dutch and English were at war. The hostilities led directly to the destruction of the Dutch East India Company.

Now the Americans sought to open the door to Asian trade. Elihu Yale, a former employee of the British East India Company in India, set up trading links with Asia. The profits led to the foundation of Yale University.

Salem, Massachusetts, became the spice centre of the world with nearly a thousand ships making the voyage from the US to the bountiful Asian ports during the 19th century. America remains the world's largest purchaser of spices, followed by Germany, Japan and France.

SPICE IN THE KITCHEN

Pungent spices were once used to disguise the taste of meat which was long past its best. Thankfully, this is no longer necessary! Today spices are used on meats, vegetables or pulses for the range of tastes they impart. The results can be fierce, musky, zesty, redolent, subtle, sweet, stinging or delicate. Our palates are becoming increasingly sophisticated, given the sheer variety of cuisine now available to us. Never has there been a better time to delve into the world of spices. It takes time and just a little knowledge to make good use of nature's hottest properties. Don't be discouraged by the mystique which surrounds spices, and has done since they first travelled away from their native lands, hundreds of years ago. Take a tour of our spice rack to learn more about the hidden qualities of those delicately coloured powders, brittle pods and diminutive seeds.

Garlic
LATIN NAME   *Allium sativum*

Like it or loathe it, garlic is in a class apart. Along with the onion it is a member of the lily family which well deserves its folk name of 'stinking rose'. But there's nothing else so versatile, that can grow in the tropics and in temperate zones; that can be fried, boiled, braised or roasted with ease; that is accredited as an antiseptic and antibiotic; and that in folklore can keep vampires, witches and other supernatural entities at bay. For those who dislike the odour, put cloves whole into a dish during cooking and remove before serving. Garlic fans will make good use of a plastic press. Keep the cloves whole so the task of cleaning the press is an easy one.

Lemon grass
LATIN NAME   *Andropogon*

Lemon grass is still something of a stranger in the west. It has been introduced to the world with the spread of Thai, Indonesian and Vietnamese cooking. Rather than the foliage it is the whitish stalks which are prized by cooks. The taste is of lemon, of course, but it gives a hint of citrus rather than carrying out a full scale assault on the senses. Although it is at home in the tropics lemon grass will grow in other hot spots, including South America, India and Australia. If it is difficult to grow or buy, substitute for a mix of lemon zest and grated ginger.

Mustard
LATIN NAME   *Brassica nigra/b. juncea/Sinapsis alba*

Mustard is made from the seeds of three different plants which are either brown, black or white. In ancient times the seeds were mixed with grape must and that is how it got its name. Mustard plants – relations of the cabbage – grow everywhere and so it was the one spice which

was accessible to most people throughout the ages. Today it is blended into numerous varieties, American mustard being among the mildest and Dijon the most powerful. For a potent spice black mustard seeds are used. Always seek fresh mustard seeds as they become bitter when they age.

Chilli Peppers
LATIN NAME   *Capsicum annuum/*
Capsicum frutescens

Chilli peppers were one of the treasures of the New World, unknown to Europe until the return of Columbus. There are numerous varieties each bearing differently shaped fruits of diverse strength ranging from mild to fiery, probably all descendants of one initial plant. It is impossible to detect just how hot a chilli will be by the smell. One of the smallest types, birdseye chilli, is the most volatile. Nutritionally they are rich in vitamins A and C and iron. When chilli is ground it becomes cayenne pepper. As a blend with capiscums and herbs it is chilli powder. In a bottle it is tabasco sauce. Handle chillies with care and always wash your hands thoroughly afterwards to get rid of the volatile oil.

Paprika
LATIN NAME   *Capsicum tertragonum*

Familiar as a rust-coloured, peppery powder, paprika is in fact dried, ground capsicum pepper, from the same family as the chilli. We know that such peppers were discovered in Mexico and taken to Spain by a succession of explorers four centuries ago. However it is not known just how they reached Hungary, the country with which paprika is most commonly associated. Apart from the Hungarian variety there is the lesser known Spanish paprika which is lighter in colour and spicier to taste. The pepper it is made from is pimiento, recognisable as the red stuffing inside Spain's green olives.

**ABOVE AND RIGHT:
CHILLI PEPPERS COME
IN MANY VARIETIES AND
RANGE FROM MILD TO
FIERY IN FLAVOUR.**

Caraway
LATIN NAME *Carum carvi*

This is probably the grandfather of all spices with a lineage that dates back to the Mesolithic times some 5,000 years ago. It was used by the early Egyptians, is mentioned in the Bible and its very name is derived from the old Arabian word 'karawya'. These days it is caraway seeds which are most commonly used, in or on top of cakes. Also, the young leaves are thought to aid digestion and even tackle diarrhoea.

Cinnamon
LATIN NAME *Cinnamomum verum/*
Cinnamomum zeylanicum

Cinnamon trees are indigenous to Sri Lanka and were first recorded by the Arab writer Kazwini in the 13th century. Mention of cinnamon in the Old Testament has caused confusion. It appears now that the Biblical writers were referring to another spice, cassia, which was a native of China. Cinnamon is taken from the bark of the evergreen cinnamon tree which grows to some 30 feet or 10 metres in height. Outer bark, which is dark and thick, is stripped off in the tropical rainy season to expose the finer bark beneath. The bark is rolled into quills which are dried in the shade to avoid warping.

Saffron
LATIN NAME *Crocus sativus*

The cost of saffron is legendary. That's because the precious sunset-stained threads are the stamens of the saffron crocus. These delicate articles are hand picked – and it takes more than 5,000 separate stamens to yield an ounce (25g) of spice. Its flavour is enhanced if it is dry-roasted before use. During history it has been used as a medicine, dye, perfume and kitchen supplement. It has always held immense value and the penalties for meddling with its qualities were severe. In 1456 Hans Kolbele was buried alive in Nuremberg after adulterating it.

Cumin
LATIN NAME *Cuminum cyminum*

Once cumin was confined to the upper regions of the Nile. Yet this hardy plant can tolerate chilly climes equally well. Cumin spice comes from the seed of this white or rose-flowered herb which is grey-green in colour and often ground for kitchen use. The Romans sprinkled cumin powder on their food in the same way we do with pepper. But the habit of using cumin in European cooking has been lost and it is now most commonly used in Indian, North African and Asian cuisine when black cumin seeds, which are darker and more sophisticated in flavour, are occasionally required. Both types should be dry-roasted before being ground.

RIGHT: CINNAMON SHAVINGS CAN BE USED IN BOTH SWEET AND SAVOURY DISHES.

BELOW: SAFFRON, THE MOST HIGHLY PRIZED SPICE, IS PAINSTAKINGLY HARVESTED FROM THE STAMENS OF THE SAFFRON CROCUS.

Turmeric
LATIN NAME *Curcuma longa*

Turmeric has a reputation as a poor man's saffron. It has similar food colouring qualities but none of the subtleties of flavour. A relation of ginger, it has that same soft bark of a skin but inside it resembles a carrot in colour. The taste is of musk and citrus with a sprinkling of pepper. Much of its quality is lost when it is ground but that is nevertheless how it is most usually found in the west. The turmeric plant has large, glossy leaves, like those of a lily, and flowers spikes clothed in pale yellow. In eastern countries it is used not only in cooking but also medicinally and for dying fabric.

Cardamom
LATIN NAME *Elettaria cardamomum*

A rainforest dweller, cardamom is at home in India and Burma where its green, oval fruits which have a score of seeds inside are used in savoury and sweet dishes. Beware of imitations. Distantly related but inferior pods from the 'Amomum' family are often used as substitutes. These hoary brown articles grown in Nepal or China lack the delicate flavour of the real thing. The difficulty of cultivating cardamom is reflected in its high cost. Cardamom seeds can be sucked as breath fresheners.

Cloves
LATIN NAME *Eugenia aromatica*

A rich flavour and a heady scent make cloves an essential addition to numerous dishes ranging from bread and cakes to meat and sweets. The cloves are like blunt pins with rounded heads. These are the unopened buds of the evergreen clove tree which once grew only in the Spice Islands. Harvested twice yearly, the buds are then dried when they assume a woody appearance. Their shape makes them ideal for studding food, like onions and the skin of ham – items which can be removed before serving. As a mouthful of cloves would be hard to bear, a specially-made infuser is another option, as is ground clove powder.

Asafoetida
LATIN NAME *Ferula asafoetida*

The most overwhelming thing about asafoetida is its dreadful smell. Sample it raw and the bitter taste may put you off it for life. It takes only a small quantity to flavour food and, thankfully, much of the odour vanishes upon cooking. The spice is the ground root or rhizome of the plant which grows as tall as a man and has yellow umbels on fleshy stems. It will keep its pungency for several years after it has been harvested. It can be purchased in lump or powder form.

Star anise

LATIN NAME *Illicium verum*

One of the most attractive spices, star anise is grown in China and predominantly used in that country's cuisine. As the name implies, it is rich with the flavour of aniseed. It comes from a tree of the magnolia family which bears greenish yellow fragrance-free flowers. When the blooms wither a brown, eight-pointed star forms, with a seed nestling inside each one. It is the pod that has most flavour, however, and it is used whole or ground with the seeds. As a spice its popularity has remained largely within China and Vietnam but it has travelled with the emigrant Chinese and is finding favour as an alternative for aniseed.

Juniper

LATIN NAME *Juniperus communis*

Long ago juniper had a greater currency than it does today. The purple-blue berries found on a compact, spiny shrub might have been roasted and brewed in place of coffee beans or ground and shaken over food instead of pepper. These uses are long forgotten but the berries are sometimes used to accompany various types of game which have a strong flavour. Perhaps its most common use is in gin, the very name of which is derived from the Dutch word for Juniper.

Galangal

LATIN NAME *Languas galanga/Alpina galanga*
L.officinarum/a.officinarum

There are two types of galangal, greater and lesser. The first is common to Indonesia while the second is native to southern China. Galangal is the root of the plant which has long, narrow leaves with white orchid-like flowers bearing red markings. It looks like ginger and indeed its uses are much the same too. It is available in dried form and can be added to stews or curries by the slice. But don't forget to remove it before serving as it is unpleasant to taste.

Curry leaves

LATIN NAME *Murraya koenigii*

This is a popular garden plant in India, the reason being that its leaves have a mouthwatering aroma of curry. It is an ornamental tree which is native to the foothills of the Himalayas. The leaves appear nothing special but, when crushed, summon up the character of a curry and are a particular asset in vegetarian cooking. Stalks of leaves are added to curries to improve the flavour. These are removed before serving. Alas, curry leaves do not dry well as much of their quality is lost in the process.

LEFT: JUNIPER BERRIES HAVE BEEN SIDELINED IN MODERN COOKERY FOR USE ONLY WITH STRONGLY FLAVOURED GAME.

DECORATIVE AND DELICIOUS, STAR ANISE IS AN ORIENTAL SPICE. BOTH POD AND SEEDS CAN BE USED WHOLE OR MAY BE GROUND INTO A GINGERY-COLOURED POWDER.

Nutmeg & Mace
LATIN NAME *Myristica fragrans*

From a single tree comes two distinct spices. Nutmeg is the fruit of the tree and the stringy kernel of the fruit is mace. Both are protected on the tree by an outer husk. They taste similar but mace has a bitter quality and lends itself to savoury dishes while nutmeg can be freshly grated onto various dishes, notably those with eggs and milk among the ingredients. Both were recognised for their medicinal qualities long before their culinary uses. Apart from easing stomach upsets they were considered aphrodisiacs and hallucinogenics.

Nigella
LATIN NAME *Nigella sativa*

Gardeners are familiar with the frilly blue finery of nigella, otherwise known as love-in-a-mist. The culinary nigella is a close relative which blooms in less spectacular fashion and produces small, black seeds which may be left whole or can be ground. Unfashionable in European cookery, nigella is used throughout the Middle East and in Indian cookery, not least to flavour nan bread. Nigella also features in several spice mixes. Its other claim to fame is as an insect repellant.

Poppy
LATIN NAME *Papaver somniferum*

The seeds are taken from the opium poppy but have none of the side-effects associated with the flower or its by-products of morphine, opium and codeine. The seeds come in different hues, from blue-black, through brown to yellow, depending on where in the world the poppy seeds were harvested. They can be used in curries or spread on bread, biscuits, salad or on other dishes as a garnish.

Allspice
LATIN NAME *Pimenta dioica*

A member of the Myrtle family allspice is the name of the small, green berries which are picked before they ripen and left to dry, either in kilns or in the sun. The name pimento comes from the Spanish for pepper because the berries resemble peppercorns. It was christened allspice as the taste is reminiscent of nutmeg, cinnamon and cloves. Most of the world's supply comes from Jamaica where the attractive trees grow in plantations known locally as Pimento walks. For optimum flavour grind allspice as required.

Anise
LATIN NAME *Pimpinella anisum*

For its distinctive flavour aniseed has long been held in high esteem. Native to the Middle East and the islands of the Eastern Mediterranean, its seed was spread with the Roman empire. Anise was used medicinally, as an aphrodisiac and as a spice. Today it is probably most widely encountered in drinks as most European nations have a favourite tipple based on its flavour. If the plant appears familiar it is because it is a relation of fennel, dill and caraway but can be distinguished by its creamy white flowers.

Cubeb
LATIN NAME *Piper cubeba*

A member of the rambling pepper family, cubebs grow in Indonesia and are in fact unripe bobble berries. Colloquially they are called tailed pepper because, although they are gravelly like peppercorns, each bearing a short stalk. It was long used as a medicine and a spice but was suppressed during the 17th century to protect the peppercorn trade. The flavour reflects allspice rather than pepper.

POPPY SEEDS ARE OFTEN USED AS A FINISHING TOUCH.

Pepper
LATIN NAME   *Piper nigrum*

The humble peppercorn was one of the driving forces of the age of exploration. So valuable was pepper that rents and ransoms were paid in it and it could be exchanged for gold, ounce for ounce. Da Gama was inspired to face the unknown in order to secure a new route to pepper, a native of India. The peppercorns are the green berries which grow on a vine. Black pepper-corns are harvested and sundried, while white pepper-corns are left to ripen on the vine and are then soaked in water to remove the outer husk revealing the pale inner. Pink peppercorns are in fact the product of a South American tree, *Schinus terehinthifolius*.

Sesame
LATIN NAME   *Sesamum indicum*

The graceful sesame plant with its soft leaves and pink or white flowers grows widely in Africa and Asia. In China, where it has been cultivated for some 2,000 years, it is still known as 'foreign hemp'. Sesame seeds come in a trio of colours – brown, black and white. They are thought to have been pressed for oil before any other seed or fruit, perhaps as early as 900 BC. Sesame is familiar to many in a ground paste known as tahina which is widely used in the Middle East and also in halva. In the west sesame seeds are toasted and put on loaves.

Sarsaparilla
LATIN NAME   *Smilax ornata*

When it arrived in Spain in the middle of the 16th century the root of sarsaparilla was hailed as a remedy for syphilis. Later it emerged as a tonic to help rheumatics and those with skin problems. The plant is a woody vine with whitish flowers which turn into berries. Today it is used as a flavouring both in the pharmaceutical industry and in soft drinks.

Tamarind
LATIN NAME   *Tamarindus indic*

The brown pod of the Tamarind tree is generally picked when it is brittle and about to split. Inside there's a seedy pulp. However, tamarind is rarely in this form when it is bought over the shop counter. Although some Asian shops sell dried pods it is usually sold in a block of peeled and seeded tamarind which must be soaked to extract the flavour. Alternatively tamarind concentrate – a blackish paste – is available, to be used in tiny quantities. Tamarind lends a fruity sour taste to food, much as lemon does. It is used in curries, hot and sour soup and, in the West Indies, in thirst-quenching drinks. Leaves from the evergreen tamarind tree contain red and yellow dyes.

Fenugreek
LATIN NAME   *Trigonella foenum-graecum*

Its primary use for years was as cattle fodder and 'green' manure. The Latin name translates to 'Greek hay'. Yet it is so intensely aromatic that Fenugreek has a valued place in commercially produced curry powder. The resilient Fenugreek plant stands about two feet or 60 centimetres high and bears yellow flowers with three leaves to a stem. Unless they are dried or roasted both foliage and seeds have a tendency to bitterness but combine well with others. Fresh green shoots can be used in salad in moderation and the yellow, square seeds can also be sprouted for salad garnish, in the same way as mustard and cress.

Vanilla
LATIN NAME   *Vanilla planifolia*

**RIGHT: GINGER HAS
WARMING QUALITIES
AND IS EQUALLY AT
HOME IN CAKES OR
CURRIES.**

**BELOW: ALTHOUGH
IT LOOKS UNPROMISING,
VANILLA EXUDES
A SWEET, LIGHT
FRAGRANCE AND TASTE.**

A commonplace flavouring but alas, most items which claim to be vanilla are in fact adulterated with cheap imitations. For vanilla is one of the most expensive spices on the market, even today when cultivation of the trailing orchid has gone far beyond its native home of Mexico. Vanilla pods are dark brown, long, supple and last for ages. Mellow and deliciously fragrant, they can be used time and again when the flavour they continue to impart will still be superior to the numerous synthetic substitutes. Store a vanilla pod in a jar of sugar for cake, pudding and chocolate making.

Wasabi
LATIN NAME   *Wasabia japonica*

A native of Japan, wasabi is to be found only in the marshy hinterlands of fast-running streams. In Japan it is known as the mountain hollyhock although in the west it has been named Japanese horseradish. Wasabi is the green pulp encased inside a tougher brown root. The flavour is hot and long-lasting. It can be grated and used fresh, dried and ground or turned into a paste. Although it is little used outside Japan it has achieved some worldwide recognition for its use in sushi, the fashionable and highly acclaimed raw fish dish.

Sichuan pepper
LATIN NAME   *Xanthoxylum piperitum*

This spice of many names is also known as fagara, anise pepper, Chinese pepper and flower pepper. Confusingly, it is not related to the plant which gives us black and white peppercorns but an ash tree native to China. Its berries are dried after being harvested then crushed. Use is mainly confined to China. Sichuan pepper is, however, closely related to Sansho, one of the Japanese spices.

Ginger
LATIN NAME   *Zingiber officinale*

The fawn-skinned and knobbly rhizome of the ginger plant looks profoundly unappetising, particularly when compared to its exotic flower. Still, centuries ago someone must have sampled the moist and softly woody root for it has long been a daily staple of Asian cuisine. Inside it has a mustard hue, although tender young ginger may appear pink. Its flavour is warm without being overpowering. For savoury and sweet dishes fresh is preferable (buy roots with a smooth, unwrinkled skin) but ground ginger is more frequently used outside the tropics. Ginger is also available pickled, as oil, in wine, in syrup and crystallised.

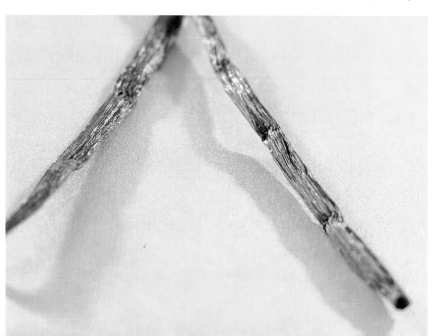

SPICE BLENDS AROUND THE WORLD

Spices are rarely used in isolation. A well-chosen selection works in harmony to produce a taste sensation which once experienced will not easily be forgotten. Spices commonly grow in hot countries and it is in their native lands that they are most widely used.

Once spice blends were employed for all manner of purposes, not all of them virtuous. The Greeks and Romans used a mixture of pepper, myrrh and perfume as an aphrodisiac. Spices were also included in the recipes for poisons which were commonly used to resolve personal conflicts during the Middle Ages. Aconite root, opium and mandrake were favourites, along with the herbs belladonna and hemlock.

Now spices are used entirely in the kitchen, and popular spice blends from different regions have come to symbolise nations' culinary expertise. The experienced eater will even be able to detect which region a meal is from by its subtle flavours. Rules are few when it comes to adding spice at home, and the connoisseur will tweak every measure until the result is tailor-made for his own taste buds.

India

The natural home of spice is surely India, where exotic and extraordinary combinations are part of everyday life.

In a country with a population of 844 million people speaking no fewer than 1600 languages and dialects the range of cuisine is astronomical. The outside influences on Indian cookery include Persian and European.

Gourmet food in southern India is almost exclusively vegetarian and its flavour is a cut above the imitations found overseas. That's because fresh spices are readily available in India whereas dried forms are used elsewhere. It is intended to make the eater break out in a sweat as a way of cooling off in the region's intense heat. Spices have huge importance in turning ordinary root crops or pulses into something special.

Curry

The stock dish in India is, of course, curry, which is now popular across the world. A curry is only as good as the curry powder used to flavour it and, if you are not happy with the results from a shop-bought variety, it is worth devoting the time and effort to making your own. Combining ingredients at home enables you to economise on your least favourite flavours and bolster up quantities of those you like best. For those who prefer excessively mild or strong curries it is the easiest and best alternative.

In essence a curry powder is a blend of dried chillies, coriander seeds, cumin seeds, mustard seeds, peppercorns, fenugreek seeds, fresh curry leaves, ground ginger and turmeric. Before grinding the whole ingredients to a powder de-seed the chillies and dry roast them with the coriander, cumin, mustard, peppercorns and fenugreek. Some recipes call for the addition of cinnamon and cloves. Just two tablespoonfuls are sufficient to flavour a curry of 3lb or 1.5 kg of vegetables. Once it is made curry powder will keep in an airtight jar for up to four months.

In Sri Lanka the chilli is left out in favour of milder cayenne pepper. Mustard and ginger are also absent although there are undertones of aniseed provided by fennel seeds and cardamoms, with a sweetness lent by cloves.

RIGHT: TRADE IS BRISK AT INDIAN SPICE MARKETS.

FAR RIGHT: WHILE WESTERNERS MAKE DO WITH A SMALL JAR OF SPICE, EASTERNERS BUY IT BY THE KILO.

Indian dishes

In northern India the role of curry powder in spicing up dishes is taken by garam masala which adds new dimensions to any onion-based sauce. It is made from cinnamon sticks, bay leaves, cumin seeds, coriander seeds, green cardamom seeds, black peppercorns, cloves and mace. Once again the whole ingredients are dry roasted before being crushed and combined with mace. Only a little is necessary to spice up a dish.

A family recipe for garam masala is handed down with pride to each new generation. The aim is to warm the body in the cooler, occasionally snowy, regions of the north so it is traditionally less savage in flavour than southern dishes.

There are regional variations of garam masala. In Kashmir they add nutmeg; for a hot Parsi Dansak masala the fiery trio of fenugreek, mustard and chillies are included. For a sour flavour, dried pomegranate seeds or anardana are among the ingredients.

Once the blend has been made it can be stored in an airtight jar away from heat and light for several months. The peril of letting it linger is that it may lose its pungency.

IN INDIA THE BLENDING OF SPICES IS A REVERED ART THROUGH WHICH GOURMET EXCELLENCE IS ACHIEVED.

Another favourite from the Punjab is tandoori in which meat is marinaded with yoghurt infused with spices including chilli, garlic, ginger, coriander seeds, cumin seeds and garam masala. As an economy on saffron and fresh turmeric the vivid colouring is these days frequently via food colourings. A milder yoghurt-

based sauce is known as korma. Bread takes the place of cutlery all over India which is why nan, chapati and poppadoms always accompany meals. These too are often subtly spiced to enhance the flavours. Lime pickle, frequently served with curries, is a mind-numbing mixture of fresh limes, hot chillies, ginger, garlic, salt, sugar and wine vinegar. Other Indian chutneys include mango, coriander, ginger and sesame.

Indians like to wake up with a glass of hot milk. Those who can afford it will still imitate the Maharajas and drink frothy milk flavoured with saffron, cardamom and slivers of pistachio.

South East Asia and Far East

In Japan there is Shichimi or seven-spice seasoning, the contents of which may vary but in essence contains red pepper flakes, ground sansho pepper (available in Japanese stores), roasted sesame seeds, roasted white poppy seeds, small pieces of orange peel, small pieces of nori (seaweed or laver) and white pepper. It is available ready-prepared in Japanese grocery shops, for sprinkling on soups, salads and noodles.

Another typically Japanese condiment is gomasio, a mixture of roasted sesame seeds and salt. The Chinese are lovers of five-spice powder, a mix of star anise, fagara, cinnamon, fennel seeds and cloves. This blend is sometimes further spiced up with cardamom, ginger or liquorice root. It is intended to combine the tastes of bitter, sweet, sour and salty and is typically used with meat or poultry.

An equivalent in Indonesia, Malaysia and Korea is the Seven Seas spice mix comprising cardamom pods, a cinnamon stick, coriander seeds, red chillies, cumin seeds, celery seeds and cloves.

It hots up in Indonesia when the favourite relish, sambal, is served. It is made mostly from chillies with just a little salt and sugar or tamarind added. Only a spoonful is needed to put a zing into soups and sauces. It can be made slightly more bland with the addition of peanuts but the end product is still extremely spicy. The recipe for sambal is modified and other ingredients added when the occasion demands.

Indonesians like a yellow mixed pickle, atjar kuning, to accompany their curries. It contains lemon grass, cumin, turmeric, cayenne pepper, coriander and garlic to pep up a selection of vegetables.

Neighbouring Thailand is equally fond of chillies. Among their national specialities is nam prik, the constituents of which are chillies, garlic, shallots, shrimp paste, peanuts, tamarind and brown sugar. For their curries they use chillies together with shallots, garlic, lemon grass, coriander root and seeds, galangal, lime peel and shrimp paste.

RIGHT: RED PEPPERS ARE DRIED IN THE SUN IN SOUTH EAST ASIA TO ENSURE A YEAR-ROUND SUPPLY.

FAR RIGHT: DRY ROAST SESAME SEEDS BEFORE USE TO BRING OUT THE FULL FLAVOUR.

Africa and the Middle East

In Northern Africa a common addition to stews and vegetables, or appearing on the table as a relish, is harissa. It's a combination of dried chillies, garlic, caraway seeds, cumin, coriander, dried mint and olive oil. It is often used to flavour couscous, a bed of which is frequently served with North African meat and fish dishes.

Morocco produces a spice mixture known as ras el hanout, put together pretty well at the discretion of the maker but usually containing a score of different dried roots, seeds and leaves. Typically ingredients include mace, allspice, cinnamon, ash berries, nigella, black pepper and cubebs. Although it makes a fragrant and attractive pot pourri it is used in cooking with game, rice, stew and sweetmeats.

Spices are ideal to flavour bland but prolific foodstuffs like dried peas and beans. In the Middle East a great favourite is felafel, chick peas ground with onion, garlic, coriander, cumin, cayenne and fresh herbs. The resulting paste is shaped into balls and deep fried.

Many countries in and around Asia have a taste for salabat, ginger tea. Ginger is warming and the Syrians add cloves, cinnamon and anise to make it even more so. Further east in Korea dried fruit is popped in while the hot tea cools so it becomes infused with flavour. In the Philippines honey is used as a sweetener. Anise tea is also popular in the Middle East. Just add boiling water to four tablespoonfuls of anise seeds and leave for several minutes. It can be served with lemon, honey or milk.

Europe and the Americas

America is a culinary crossroads where east meets west. Numerous recipes have been transported there with immigrants drawn from across the globe. The influences of Chinese, African, West Indian, French and British cuisine remain strong.

RIGHT: BARBECUED FOOD IS SPICED UP WITH A MARINADE.

BELOW: CHRISTMAS CAKES ARE FLAVOURED WITH SPICE BLENDS.

In Louisiana the prevailing taste is for Cajun cooking in which a seasoning might contain garlic, onion, paprika, black pepper and dried cumin, mustard and cayenne along with dried thyme and oregano.

For those with plainer tastes the barbecue mixes are frequently used to add an extra dimension to meat. Here herbs are used in harmony with spices, for example parsley and chives alongside paprika and mint, thyme and tarragon with lashings of black pepper.

In the Caribbean the quaintly-named Jamaican jerk seasoning is popular. Made of chillies, spring onions, shallots, garlic, chives, ginger, allspice, pepper, cinnamon, cloves and fresh thyme blended with sunflower oil, it can also be used on meat or fish for barbecues, for frying or grilling.

Old-fashioned cookery books sometimes call for kitchen pepper. This was a blend of black, white and dried green peppercorns to which cubebs, allspice, coriander and cloves were sometimes added.

For charcuterie the French use quatre-epices which comprises peppercorns, nutmeg, cloves and ginger.

For English cooking tie a selection of spices in a muslin bag and use them in pickling to flavour the vinegar. Pickling spices include mustard seeds, cloves, allspice, peppercorns and others. Italian seasoning, made from dried bay leaves, oregano, sage, thyme, pepper and paprika, goes especially well with tomato dishes.

For puddings and cakes many western recipes demand mixed spice, a blend of cinnamon, cloves, mace, nutmeg and allspice. They, and others, can be blended according to taste. Mixed spice features in well-loved recipes including Christmas cake and plum pudding. It's an important ingredient in the making of gingerbread men when mixed spice is used to complement the flavour of ginger. Use mixed spice and it is likely to be the same recipe that would have been followed in an English kitchen 400 years ago. Few culinary traditions have endured for so long in this country.

Seasoning salt, used for marinading meat, is soon made by combining sea salt with ground celery seeds, white pepper, cumin and paprika or cayenne pepper.

In the colder climates spices are particularly welcome for their warming qualities. After a bracing winter walk there is no finer welcome than a glass of steaming gluhwein; heated and spiced wine. The spices involved are dried cinnamon, root ginger, allspice berries and whole cloves, all in generous quantities. There are many different recipes but most include slices of orange and lemon and sugar in the warmed-up wine.

Herbs and spices around the house

Capitalise on the inimitable fragrance of herbs and spices by using them throughout the home in pot-pourri, herb pillows and lavender bags.

RIGHT AND FAR RIGHT: POT-POURRI BRINGS THE FRESHNESS OF THE COUNTRYSIDE INTO THE HOME.

BELOW: ESSENTIAL OILS ARE EXTRACTED FROM PLANTS FOR USE IN AROMATHERAPY.

Pot-pourri comprises a variety of flowers, leaves, seeds and spices which are then combined with a fixative that helps them endure. All scented flowers apart from those with thick, fleshy petals like lilies and hyacinth may be used. The choices can include honeysuckle, jasmine, roses, rosemary, stocks, sweet peas and wallflowers. The leaves of bay, bergamot, thyme, verbena, lavender and sage are among those which can be added, along with aromatic spices like cinnamon, cloves, coriander, allspice and aniseed. The fixatives are gum benzoin, orris root powder and salt.

It comes in two forms, dry or moist. Dry is easier to make but has a shorter lifespan. The constituents are dried and mixed, often in stages as the season progresses. In moist pot-pourri the blooms are harvested, dried and then stored tightly packed in salt away from heat and light until all the ingredients are ready for mixing.

Use specially designed pot-pourri holders which protect from moisture and dust but allow the delightful smell to circulate through slitted lids. Other variations to the theme are lavender bags and herb pillows.

English lavender (*L. angustifolia* and *L. x intermedia*) is believed to be the best for cutting and drying. After cutting lavender stems on a dry morning hang them to dry in a light, airy place protected by a paper bag for about two weeks, before filling muslim bags with the sweet-scented flowers for use all over the house.

Herb pillows are for use in the bedroom and not only make the linen smell fresh but are thought to improve sleep, too. Any fragrant grass, foliage or flower may be used. Lavender, rosemary and aniseed fragrances are traditionally associated with sound sleep.

Fresh and dry herbs have ornamental value. Bunches of fresh herbs hanging out to dry will give even the most modern kitchen that farmhouse feel. It is unlikely that these will have a culinary use afterward because they will be damaged by kitchen condensation.

GLOSSARY

Umbels: Umbrella-shaped heads of tiny flowers typical of the umbelliferae family of plants which includes angelica, caraway, chervil, coriander, dill, fennel and parsley as well as the vegetables carrot, celery and parsnip.

Dry roasted: A culinary technique to extract the full flavour and aroma of spices. Heat a heavy frying pan then add the chosen spices. Return the pan to the heat and stir frequently using a wooden spatula to avoid burning. Allow the spices to cool before grinding.

Chlorophyll: The green pigment in plants which enables them to trap the energy of sunlight.

Oxalic acid: Colourless potassium and sodium salts which are poisonous in large quantities. Oxalic acid is so strong it could be used as a metal cleaner or textile bleacher.

Perennial: A plant which endures numerous seasons.

Annual: A plant which dies after a single season.

Biennial: A plant which flowers in its second year then dies.

Passover: The Jewish festival which commemorates the Exodus from Egypt.

Pestle and mortar: A small club-shaped instrument used to pound small quantities of foodstuffs in a bowl.

INDEX